ESCAPE ROOM ADVENTURES

The Hunt for
AGENT 9

Written by Alex Woolf

Illustrated by Sian James

ARCTURUS

ARCTURUS

This edition published in 2023 by Arcturus Publishing
Limited
26/27 Bickels Yard, 151–153 Bermondsey Street,
London SE1 3HA

Author: Alex Woolf
Illustrator: Sian James
Editor: Violet Peto
Designer: Sarah Fountain
Design Manager: Jessica Holliland
Managing Editor: Joe Harris

ISBN: 978-1-3988-2579-6
CH010112NT
Supplier 29, Date 0223, PI 00002512

Printed in China

Welcome to Escape Room Adventures!

In this story, you'll be taking on the role of globe-trotting superspy Madison Blair—an agent of E.A.G.L.E., the Espionage Agency for Global Law Enforcement. You will encounter other agents in this book who will help you in your endeavours. So grab your high-tech gadgets, dust off your trench coat and trilby, and get ready for a thrilling adventure!

Your nemesis is the diabolical supervillain Agent 9. A former member of E.A.G.L.E., he continues to use his agent number to mock the people he has betrayed. Now he is head of T.H.O.R.N. (the Transnational Headquarters of the Organization for Revenge and Notoriety), a network of criminals intent on sowing chaos and overthrowing the world's governments.

Your mission, should you choose to accept it, is to capture the villain and shut down his plot ... before it's too late!

How to read this book

Unlike most books, you won't be reading this one from front to back. You must find your own route through the book to solve the mystery. For each puzzle, you are offered three or four possible solutions. Once you think you know the correct one, turn to the entry indicated in the text and see if you're right. Use your skills of observation, lateral thinking, and logic to uncover clues and solve the mysteries. The illustrations are packed with information, so keep your eyes peeled!

Difficulty levels

Choose your difficulty level, then race against the clock to solve the mystery!

ROOKIE AGENT: You have two and a half hours to solve all the puzzles. You also have five lives, which means you're allowed to get the answers wrong up to four times.

SEASONED SPY: You have two hours to solve all the puzzles, and just four lives. Get more than three answers wrong, and you have to start again!

MASTER OF ESPIONAGE: You have just one hour and a half to solve all the puzzles, and three lives, so you can't afford to make any mistakes!

Secret symbols

Look out for these symbols to help you solve the puzzles:

If you see an object marked with this symbol, take a picture with your camera pen, as you need to remember it for later.

If you see a person marked with this symbol, remember them, as you'll have to find them again later.

This time-stop symbol buys you an extra five minutes of puzzle-solving time—should you need it!

Substitution codes

You will need to decode messages in this book.

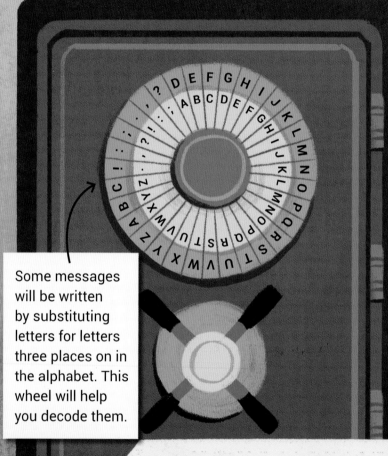

Some messages will be written by substituting letters for letters three places on in the alphabet. This wheel will help you decode them.

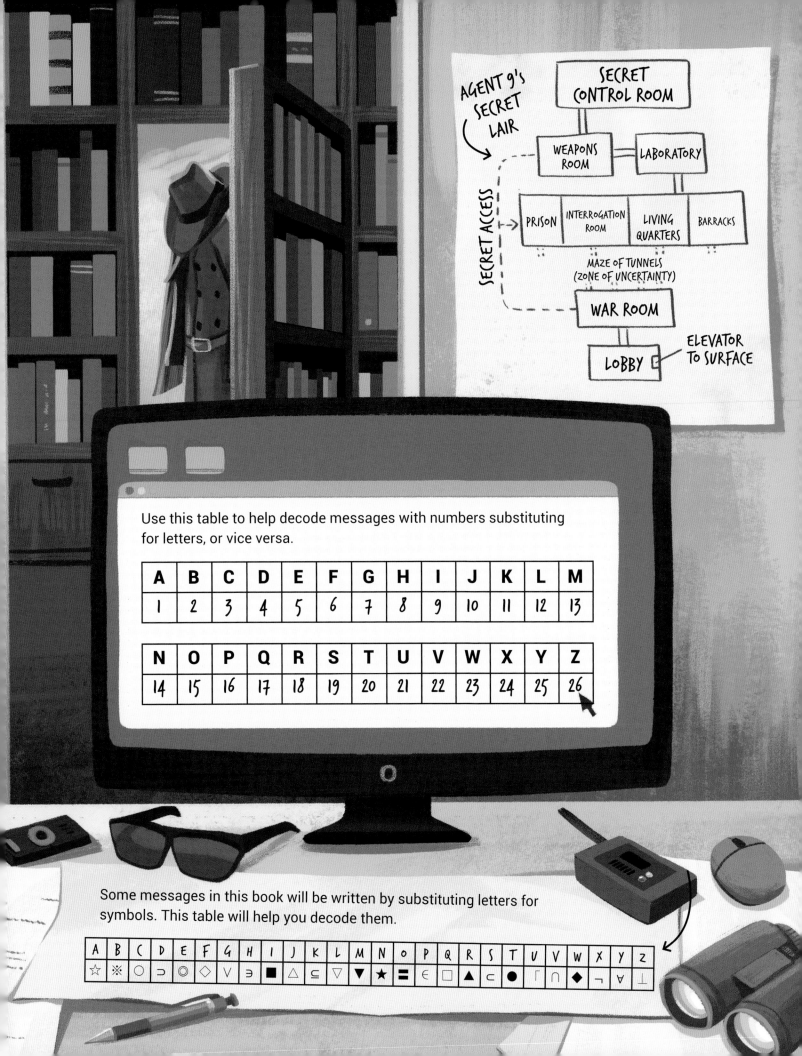

Use this table to help decode messages with numbers substituting for letters, or vice versa.

A	B	C	D	E	F	G	H	I	J	K	L	M
1	2	3	4	5	6	7	8	9	10	11	12	13

N	O	P	Q	R	S	T	U	V	W	X	Y	Z
14	15	16	17	18	19	20	21	22	23	24	25	26

Some messages in this book will be written by substituting letters for symbols. This table will help you decode them.

1 The disaster is all over the news. An earthquake has struck an uninhabited Pacific island—an earthquake so powerful that the island has been completely liquefied! Scientists are unable to explain the incident. Then, a leering face appears on every screen in the world, interrupting broadcasts. It is Agent 9!

> I am sure you are impressed by the power of my earthquake bomb. In three days, my T.H.O.R.N. agents will use those bombs to destroy world-famous monuments. That is, unless 20 billion dollars is paid into my bank account.

A

B

C

D

You have three days to find Agent 9. Your first clue: You recognize something in the background of the screen during his broadcast. It's part of a building.

Can you work out which of these buildings is behind Agent 9?

If your answer is A, turn to entry 77.

If your answer is B, turn to entry 124.

If your answer is C, turn to entry 23.

If your answer is D, turn to entry 185.

2 You won't find the book you're looking for on that shelf. Lose a life, and flip back to entry 155.

3 That is not the shape of the sea cave's mouth. Lose a life, and swim back to entry 8.

4 That is not what the agent is wearing. Lose a life, and head back to entry 190.

5 You identify the real Astra. She hands you a coded message and tells you there is no time to lose. The Great Pyramid will be blown up in two hours and twelve minutes. Which of these routes will get you there in time?

The red route is 50 km. The average speed is 25 km per hour.

The green route is 36 km. The average speed is 12 km per hour.

The blue route is 45 km. The average speed is 18 km per hour.

If your answer is the red route, turn to entry 190.

If your answer is the green route, turn to entry 39.

If your answer is the blue route, turn to entry 67.

6 The bomb is not hidden in that location on the map. Lose a life, and navigate your way back to entry 199.

7 The fingerprint does not belong to Ridley Crow. Lose a life, and return to entry 152.

8

You have identified the boat used by Agent 9, but you must act quickly. There are now only three more hours before the bomb goes off.

You search the boat thoroughly and find an old, stained picture of the mouth of a sea cave. You travel along the coast.
Which of these cave mouths looks like the one in the picture?

A

B

C

D

If you think it's A, turn to entry 3.
If you think it's B, turn to entry 58.
If you think it's C, turn to entry 164.
If you think it's D, turn to entry 70.

9
That message is incorrect. Lose a life, and recode your way back to entry 79.

10
You may need to brush up on your jigsaw puzzle skills! That is not the symbol on the broken tile. Lose a life, and return to entry 29.

11

Good choice! You run to the luggage rack where you hide just in time.

After Agent 9 has gone, you return to Ridley Crow.
He shows you a photo of the bomb at Machu Picchu,
but there's a piece missing. Can you identify it?

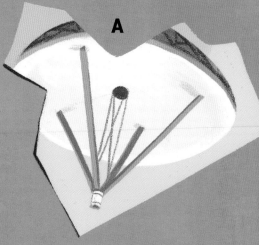

A

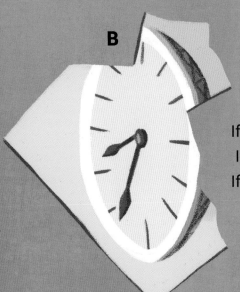

B

If you think it's A, turn to entry 100.
If you think it's B, turn to entry 78.
If you think it's C, turn to entry 204.

C

12 That number will not deactivate the bomb. Lose a life, and blast your way back to entry 120.

13 Kangaroo Airlines will not get you there the quickest, unfortunately. Lose a life, and hop back to entry 93.

14 That fuse does not lead to the dynamite. Lose a life, and untangle your way back to entry 177.

15

You have correctly decoded the message. It is a description of the T.H.O.R.N. agent who will plant the bomb. Which square is the T.H.O.R.N. agent in?

If you think they're in square A, turn to entry 102.

If you think they're in square B, turn to entry 195.

If you think they're in square C, turn to entry 64.

16 The man in the mask is not Benji Delavega. Lose a life, and head back to entry 86.

17 That is not the bomb deactivation code. Lose a life, and detonate yourself back to entry 44.

18

You have successfully decoded the note. Agent 9's next target is the Great Pyramid of Giza, in Egypt. You have no information about when the bomb is due to detonate.

You decide to call Astra Celeste in case she knows anything. However, the letters of all the names in your contacts have been jumbled up. Agent 9 must have sabotaged your phone back at the Taj Mahal.
Can you work out which of these names is an anagram of Astra Celeste?

If you think it's Tracee Stales, turn to entry 180.
If you think it's Claretta Steel, turn to entry 130.
If you think it's Ariel Cassette, turn to entry 28.
If you think it's Lisa Etcetera, turn to entry 73.

19
That path is not going to take you to the exit. Lose a life, and search for a way back to entry 51.

20
Alpaca Air is not the quickest flight to Peru. Lose a life, and jet back to entry 148.

You introduce yourself to the man. His name is Ridley Crow. He hands you an envelope containing a photograph of the next monument on Agent 9's hit list. Unfortunately, it has been cut into strips. Can you work out the order of strips and decode the secret message to identify the monument?

Which of these monuments is it?

If you think it's Christ the Redeemer in Brazil, turn to entry 182.

If you think it's the Taj Mahal Palace in India, turn to entry 111.

If you think it's the Arc de Triomphe in France, turn to entry 149.

22 Those are not the correct coordinates. Lose a life, and find your way back to entry 131.

23 That is not the correct building. Lose a life, and go back to entry 1.

24 That is not the Taj Mahal. Lose a life, and whirl back to entry 141.

25

You manage to work out the combination and open the handcuffs. You see an envelope on the seat next to you, and put it in your pocket.

At a stop light, you escape. Manuel gives chase. At Lake Titicaca, you jump aboard a reed boat. Manuel follows you in another. If Manuel's boat is going at 4 kph, and yours is going at 3 kph and you are 0.25 km ahead, at what point will he catch up with you?

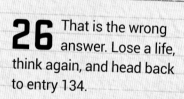

26 That is the wrong answer. Lose a life, think again, and head back to entry 134.

If your answer is 15 minutes, turn to entry 199.
If your answer is 10 minutes, turn to entry 30.
If your answer is 20 minutes, turn to entry 76.
If your answer is 25 minutes, turn to entry 158.

27 Taking a taxi is not the fastest way of getting to your destination. Lose a life, and drive back to entry 40.

28 That is not an anagram of Astra Celeste. Lose a life, and return to entry 18.

29 You find the right tile and push open a secret door into another room, where Ridley Crow is being held prisoner. You greet each other warmly.

There are three more doors. Two lead to death traps, one leads to safety.
Mend the broken tile to identify the symbol on the "safe" door.

A   B   C

If you think it's A, turn to entry 189.
If you think it's B, turn to entry 51.
If you think it's C, turn to entry 10.

30 That is the wrong answer. Lose a life, and punt your way back to entry 25.

31 That is not the car's registration number. Lose a life, and drive back to entry 111.

32

Phew! You have stopped the bomb going off. But Agent 9 isn't defeated yet. You ask your prisoner, whose name is Rochelle Blake, about the next target.

She says she doesn't know.
She's only been told the vowels
that appear in the target's name.
There's an "I", an "A", and two "U"s.

If you think it's Buckingham Palace, turn to entry 119.

If you think it's Machu Picchu, turn to entry 148.

If you think it's the Roman Forum, turn to entry 50.

If you think it's the Burj Khalifa, turn to entry 197.

33 That is not the location of the bomb. Lose a life, and blast back to entry 199.

34 You need to work on your calculating skills! Lose a life, and return to entry 107.

35 That message is not correctly coded. Manuel will know you're a fake! Lose a life, and translate yourself back to entry 79.

36

**You reach the prison by the quickest route.
On the way, you manage to steal a set of keys from a guard.**

**Astra Celeste is in one of the cells, but she looks different.
Can you recognize her among the other prisoners?**

If you think she is A, turn to entry 106.
If you think she is B, turn to entry 48.
If you think she is C, turn to entry 134.
If you think she is D, turn to entry 165.

37 That is not the quickest route to Machu Picchu. Lose a life, and head back down to entry 47.

38 The briefcase won't open using that combination. Lose a life, and go back to entry 61.

39 That route will not get you to the Great Pyramid in time. Lose a life, and head back to entry 5.

40 You take the quickest flight to Sydney and land on schedule. Now you need to get to the Opera House, pronto. You check transport alternatives. What is the quickest route to your destination? Bus, train, or taxi?

Taxi: 10-minute wait, 18-minute journey (add 10 minutes due to construction work on Macquarie Street), then a 7-minute walk.

Bus: 5-minute wait, 35-minute journey, then a 6-minute walk.

Train: 7-minute wait, 25-minute journey, then a 12-minute walk.

If you decide to take a taxi, turn to entry 27
If you decide to take the bus, turn to entry 146
If you decide to take the train, turn to entry 103

41 That is not where Agent 9 is sitting. Lose a life, and track back to entry 97.

42 The Golden Gate Bridge is not Agent 9's next target. Lose a life, and return to entry 114.

43 That person is not Agent 9. Lose a life, and return to entry 196.

44

You have found the correct book: *The Adventures of Tom Sawyer*. Tucked inside its pages is a photo to help you find the bomb hidden in the Taj Mahal, plus some clues to help you deactivate it.

Using the clues, see if you can work out the deactivation code.

BOMB DEACTIVATION CODE

☐ ☐ ☐ ☐ ☐

The third digit is three times the second digit.

The sum of the first and third digits is 14.

The fourth digit is half the third digit.

The five digits are all different and their sum is 26.

If you think the code is 82637, turn to entry 141.

If you think the code is 23946, turn to entry 200.

If you think the code is 62845, turn to entry 17.

If you think the code is 91326, turn to entry 85.

45

That is not the boat's name. Lose a life, and row back to entry 203.

46

St. Basil's Cathedral is not the next target. Lose a life, and go back to entry 187.

47 You've seen that Ridley Crow has damaged Agent 9's phone, preventing him from setting off the bomb by remote control. However, the satellite is still due to detonate the bomb at 6 pm.

You reach Cusco and there are just four hours left to get to Machu Picchu and disable the bomb. What is the quickest route?

A Taxi to Poroy (20 minutes); train to Aguas Calientes (3 hours, 15 minutes); shuttle bus to Machu Picchu (25 minutes). Turn to entry 37.

B Taxi to airport (20 minutes); wait for flight (3 hours, 5 minutes); helicopter to Machu Picchu (40 minutes). Turn to entry 174.

C Train to Ollantaytambo (2 hours); train to Aguas Calientes (90 minutes); shuttle bus to Machu Picchu (25 minutes). Turn to entry 120.

48 You have failed to recognize the real Astra Celeste. Lose a life, check your eyesight, and head back to entry 36.

49 Those are not the correct coordinates. Navigate your way back to entry 131.

50 That is not Agent 9's next target. Lose a life, and return to entry 32.

Success! You chose the right door. Now you and Ridley find yourselves in an underground labyrinth. Armed guards are ready to ambush you at every corner. What route should you take to avoid any guards?

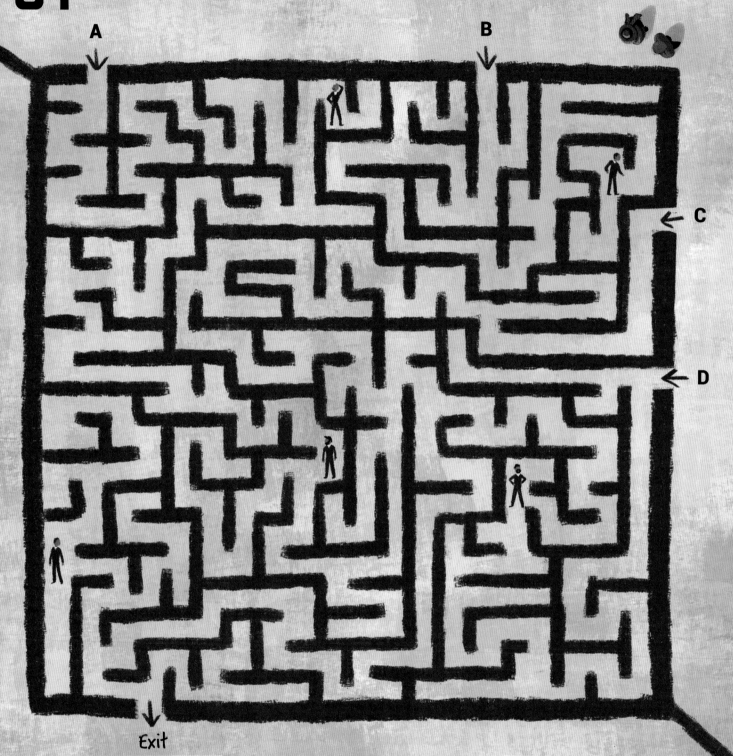

A

B

C

D

Exit

If your answer is A, turn to entry 112.

If your answer is B, turn to entry 60.

If your answer is C, turn to entry 155.

If your answer is D, turn to entry 19.

52 Climbing out of the window won't save you. Lose a life, and clamber back down to entry 169.

53 That combination will not open your handcuffs. Lose a life, and puzzle your way back to entry 183.

54

You've worked out the coordinates of Agent 9's secret lair. You jump on a helicopter to Greenland and make your way to the lair. But before you can enter it, you need a disguise to get past the guards. You disguise yourself as one of Agent 9's assistants, Rochelle Blake. Can you remember which one of these is her?

If you think it's A, turn to entry 98.

If you think it's B, turn to entry 115.

If you think it's C, turn to entry 138.

55
That is not the right answer. Lose a life, and recalculate your way back to entry 72.

56
You've failed with that combination. The briefcase's secrets remain hidden. Lose a life, and return to entry 61.

57
That is not Agent 9 you're seeing through the window. Lose a life, and creep very carefully back to entry 82.

58

You have found the cave, but time is slipping away. In two hours, the bomb will explode. Inside the cave, you find an old chest. You break it open and find bomb-making tools inside, plus a map of the island. The map shows where the bomb is located. There are two clues to its coordinates. The letter is six letters back from the first letter of the main town on Easter Island. The number is the answer to the following problem: 5 × 4 + 8 ÷ 2 − 1.

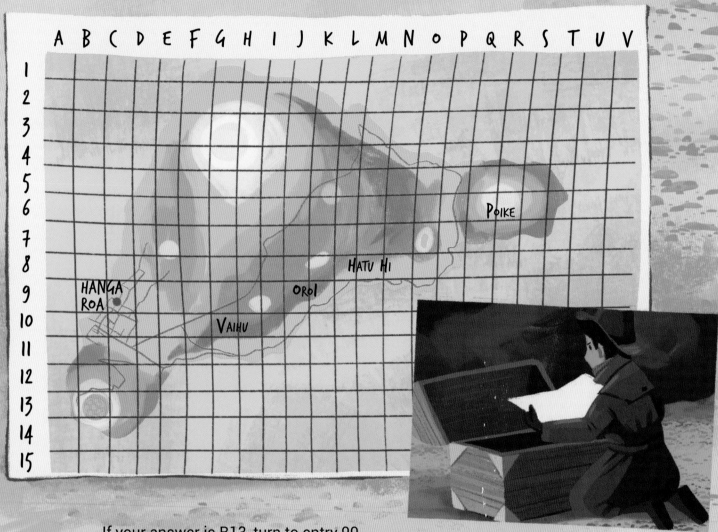

If your answer is B13, turn to entry 90.

If your answer is N5, turn to entry 172.

If your answer is E6, turn to entry 135.

59
That person is not Agent 9. Lose a life, and return to entry 196.

60
You may need to work on your maze puzzle skills! Lose a life, and find your way back to entry 51.

61

You've passed Astra's logic test. Now she's ready to tell you what she knows. She tells you that T.H.O.R.N. agents have planted the bomb to destroy the next monument. A laser satellite beam from space will trigger it. You will need to find the monument first, and then the bomb.

Astra has stolen a briefcase from Agent 9, containing the name of the next target.
Can you work out the 3-number combination that will open it?

This is what Astra knows about the code:

319 Only one of these digits is right, but it's in the wrong place.

658 Only one of these digits is right, and it's in the right place.

385 All of these digits are wrong.

714 Only one of these digits is right, and it's in the right place.

If your answer is 513, turn to entry 137.
If your answer is 846, turn to entry 38.
If your answer is 947, turn to entry 56.
If your answer is 694, turn to entry 114

62
The fingerprint does not belong to Astra Celeste. Lose a life, and go back to entry 152.

63
That is not the correct number. Lose a life, and phone back to entry 100.

64 You find the bomber. She is about to escape, but then Astra appears and blocks her path. You and Astra capture the enemy agent, but her bomb is still timed to go off in the next six minutes, unless you can deactivate it.

You study the bomb. To stop it going off, you need to work out the next shape in the pattern sequence.

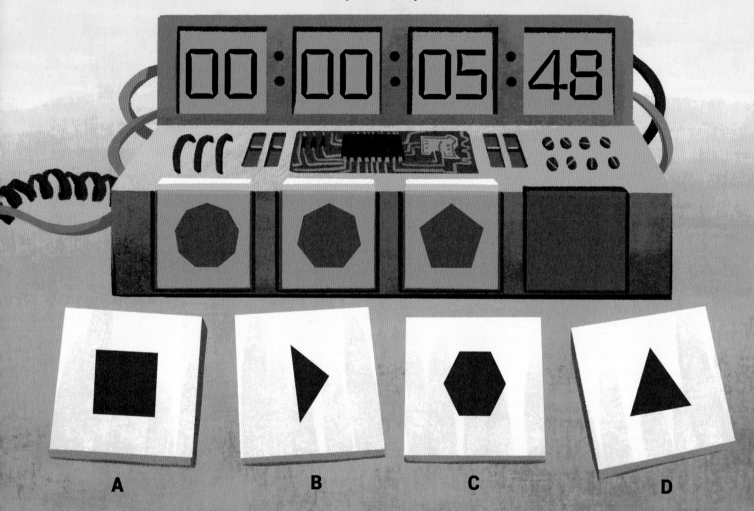

A   **B**   **C**   **D**

If your answer is A, turn to entry 99.

If your answer is B, turn to entry 143.

If your answer is C, turn to entry 206.

If your answer is D, turn to entry 32.

65 That is not the odd tile. Look again! Lose a life, and head back to entry 163.

66 The Great Wall of China is not Agent 9's next target. Lose a life, and return to entry 114.

67 That route will not get you to the bomb site in time. Lose a life, and blast your way back to entry 5.

68

You reach the Living Quarters and are about to head into the Laboratory when you hear knocks on the wall from the prison. You recognize the pattern of the knock. It's Astra Celeste. You want to rescue her, but you only have 10 minutes left before Agent 9 fires his satellite laser, activating an earthquake bomb and wiping out the next target on his list.

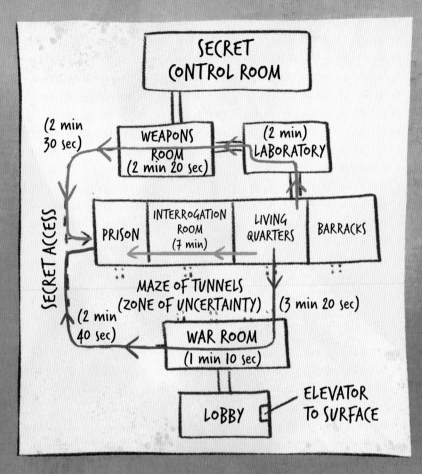

Which of these routes will get you to the prison fastest?

BLUE Go via the LABORATORY, WEAPONS ROOM, and SECRET ACCESS PASSAGE.

YELLOW Talk your way past the door guard.

RED Go via the MAZE OF TUNNELS, WAR ROOM, and SECRET ACCESS PASSAGE.

If you think it's BLUE, turn to entry 36.

If you think it's YELLOW, turn to entry 147.

If you think it's RED, turn to entry 94.

---

69 The Parthenon is the wrong monument! Lose a life, and decipher your way back to entry 187.

70 That does not look like the cave mouth in the picture. Lose a life, and go back to entry 8.

71 That is not Astra Celeste. Lose a life, and disguise your way back to entry 180.

72

You send the message to Manuel's phone. You watch him read it and leave the station. Ten minutes later, you join Agent 9 aboard the train.

Agent 9 tells you the bomb will explode at 6 pm tomorrow evening. It is now 12 noon. The train will reach Cusco in 8 hours; there is a 13-hour stopover in Cusco. Then the bus to Machu Picchu takes 5 hours.

How much time will that leave you at Machu Picchu to find and disable the bomb?

If you think it's 2 hours, turn to entry 123.
If you think it's 4 hours, turn to entry 82.
If you think it's 3 hours, turn to entry 55.

73 That is not an anagram of Astra Celeste. Lose a life, and unjumble your way back to entry 18.

74 That is not the car's registration number. Lose a life, and take a spin back to entry 111.

75 You have found your way down the wall of the crater to the bomb. To deactivate it, you must solve this mathematical riddle. But be quick about it. In just nine minutes, the bomb will go off!

Work out what combination of +, −, × and ÷ will make sense of this equation ...

If your answer is +, −, ×, ÷, turn to entry 167.

If your answer is ×, ÷, −, +, turn to entry 80.

If your answer is ÷, +, ×, −, turn to entry 122.

If your answer is −, ×, +, ÷, turn to entry 144.

76 That is the wrong answer. Lose a life, and make your way back to entry 25.

77 That was not the correct building. Lose a life, and go back to entry 1.

78 That is not the correct missing piece of the photograph. Lose a life, and snap back to entry 11.

79 You disguise yourself as Manuel Malado and meet Agent 9 at the railway station. He's taken in by your disguise, but then the real Manuel appears. He hasn't seen you or Agent 9.

You need to send Manuel away before Agent 9 sees him. You secretly use your watch to hack Agent 9's phone contacts for Manuel's number. You need to send him some new orders in Agent 9's code: "Change of plan. Meet at two pm instead."

How should you write this?

FKDQJH RI SODQ. PHHW DW WZR DP LQVWHDG. Turn to entry 126.
FKDQJH RI SODQ. PHHW DW RQH DP LQVWHDG. Turn to entry 35.
FKDQJH RI SODQ. PHHW DW RQH SP LQVWHDG. Turn to entry 9.
FKDQJH RI SODQ. PHHW DW WZR SP LQVWHDG. Turn to entry 72.

80 That combination will not produce the correct answer. Lose a life, and subtract yourself back to entry 75.

81 That is not the correct snowflake design. Lose a life, and drift back to entry 117.

82 You've worked out that you will have four hours to disable the bomb. You start to relax, but then Agent 9 receives a call from Manuel Malado. Realizing you are an imposter, he pulls off your disguise.

He draws a gun and forces you out of a train window, but you cling on. You edge along the side of the train to a window, and see a familiar silhouette inside. Who is it?

If you think it's Ridley Crow, turn to entry 169.

If you think it's Manuel Malado, turn to entry 142.

If you think it's Agent 9, turn to entry 57.

83 That is not the correct answer. Lose a life, and calculate your way back to entry 120.

84 That is the wrong woman! Do not approach her. Lose a life, and go back to entry 173.

85 That is not the correct bomb deactivation code. Lose a life, and explode back to entry 44.

86 You chose the correct flight! Unfortunately, Rochelle Blake managed to send a message to her contact in Puno. He captures you as you emerge from the airport, and pushes you into his car. He is wearing a mask, so you can only see part of his face. Which of Agent 9's assistants does he resemble?

Manuel Malado

Benji Delavega

Freddy Ravelo

If you think it's Manuel Malado, turn to entry 183.
If you think it's Benji Delavega, turn to entry 16.
If you think it's Freddy Ravelo, turn to entry 128.

87 You may need to work on your decoding skills! Lose a life, and return to entry 103.

88 That combination will not gain you entry into Agent 9's lair. Lose a life, and go back to entry 138.

89 That is not the man you are looking for in the park. Lose a life, and take a stroll back to entry 144.

90

You've figured out that the bomb is hidden inside the crater of a volcano called Rano Kau. If it goes off, it could cause a major landslide that will destroy many of the island's moai. It is due to detonate in under one hour.

When you reach the volcano's crater, you find a tangle of ropes to get down there. Which one takes you to the bottom, where the bomb is?

If your answer is A, turn to entry 96.

If your answer is B, turn to entry 113.

If your answer is C, turn to entry 75.

91 That is not the correct order for the film stills. Lose a life, and remix your way back to entry 127.

92 That is not where the bomb is hidden. Lose a life, and return to entry 166.

93

You are right! The building is the Sydney Opera House in Australia. Agent 9 said he would destroy the next monument in three days, so there's no time to lose. You check flights from New York, USA, to Sydney, Australia. Which will get you there the quickest? Each journey takes 23 hours, *not including* the stop at Los Angeles International Airport (LAX).

DEPARTURES

Airline	Departs	Stop at LAX
Skyline	6 pm	54 mins
Gamma Airways	5.45 pm	1 hr 13 mins
Breezy Air	6.05 pm	52 mins
Kangaroo Airlines	5.55 pm	1 hr

If your answer is Skyline, turn to entry 40.

If your answer is Gamma Airways, turn to entry 129.

If your answer is Breezy Air, turn to entry 192.

If your answer is Kangaroo Airlines, turn to entry 13.

---

94 That is not the quickest route to the prison. Lose a life, and find your way back to entry 68.

95 You have not decoded the message correctly. Lose a life, and head back to entry 103.

96 That rope will not get you to the bottom of the volcano's crater. Lose a life, and climb back to entry 90.

97

You manage to call the police and they evacuate the site. Now you must stop Agent 9 from setting off the bomb by remote control.

You use your tracker app to see if you can locate Agent 9. Can you work out his carriage, row, and seat number from this diagram?

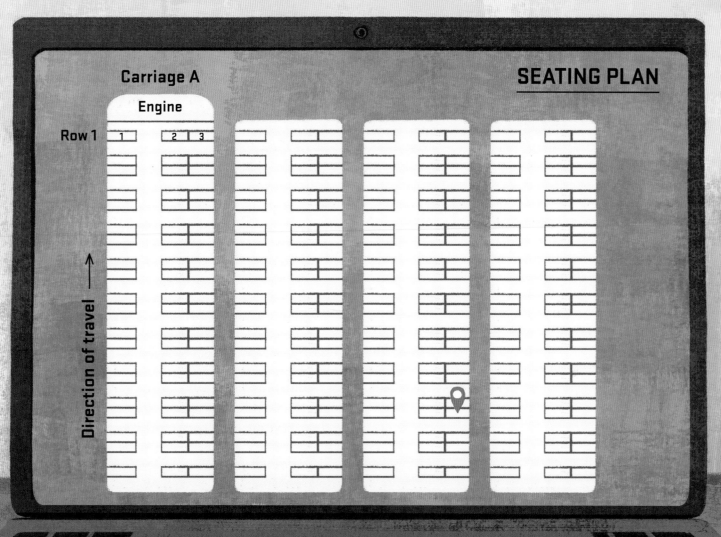

If you think he's in Carriage C, Row 17, Seat 3, turn to entry 127.
If you think he's in Carriage B, Row 16, Seat 3, turn to entry 41.
If you think he's in Carriage C, Row 15, Seat 2, turn to entry 170.
If you think he's in Carriage A, Row 18, Seat 2, turn to entry 110.

98 That is not Rochelle Blake. Lose a life, redisguise yourself, and return to entry 54.

99 That is not the next shape in the pattern sequence. Lose a life, and reason your way back to entry 64.

100

The missing piece is a satellite receiver dish, so the bomb can be detonated by remote control. This means Agent 9 could set it off now if he wanted to.

You would like to call the police in Cusco to warn them to evacuate the site, but Agent 9 has used a scrambler device to jumble up all the numbers on your phone. Use the following clues to work out the correct number order:

- The numbers go odd, odd, even, even, odd, even, even, odd, odd.

- The third number is higher than the second number, but lower than the first number.

- The fourth number is half of the third number, and double the seventh number.

Which is the correct number?

734258619: turn to entry 118.

918436257: turn to entry 97.

526391478: turn to entry 63.

358492675: turn to entry 178.

101
That is the wrong answer. Lose a life, dust off those brain cells, and head back to entry 134.

102
The agent isn't in that square. Lose a life, and head back to entry 15.

103

You've chosen the quickest route to the Sydney Opera House. As you are walking toward it, someone bumps into you. You look around and see a woman walking away from you. You check your pocket in case she stole your wallet. In there, you find a note written in code. Can you decode it?

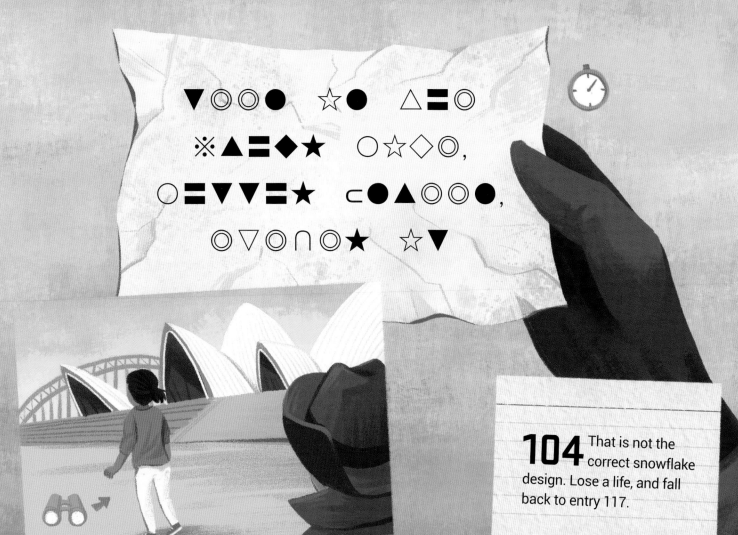

Which of these should you do?

A Make your way to General Street.

B Get ready for a rendezvous at eleven am.

C Go to the John Black Café.

D Set off for Standard Street.

If your answer is A, turn to entry 87.

If your answer is B, turn to entry 173.

If your answer is C, turn to entry 205.

If your answer is D, turn to entry 95.

104

That is not the correct snowflake design. Lose a life, and fall back to entry 117.

105

No, that's not the agent. Lose a life, and go back to entry 144.

106

That is not Astra Celeste. Lose a life, and go back to entry 36.

107

You identify the woman and go and speak to her. She tells you her name is Astra Celeste. She claims she used to work for T.H.O.R.N. and has some information about Agent 9. She wants to help you defeat him, but it's going to be a challenge, and first she wants to verify that your logical skills are up to scratch.

She sets you a puzzle. The blue arrows represent addition. The orange arrows represent multiplication. Can you work out the puzzle? What number should be in the circle with the question mark?

If your answer is 28, turn to entry 175.
If your answer is 32, turn to entry 61.
If your answer is 16, turn to entry 34.
If your answer is 26, turn to entry 140.

108 That is not the correct order of film stills. Lose a life, and rearrange your way back to entry 127.

109 That is a famous building, but it's not being targeted by Agent 9. Lose a life, and return to entry 124.

110 That is not where Agent 9 is sitting. Lose a life, and head back to entry 97.

111 You work out that the monument is the Taj Mahal in India. You and Ridley take a flight to Delhi. As you emerge from the airport, you hear the screech of tires. You turn and see a car driving away. Ridley has been captured! You must try and track down the car, but you only caught a glimpse of the registration as it sped off.

This is what you remember:

There is a D.
The final four characters are numbers in descending order.

You check the local registration database for cars matching the description in the area at the time, and narrow it down to four possibilities.

Which registration is it?
D 24 R 1459: Turn to entry 31.
LH 15 D 6423: Turn to entry 198.
DL 06 C 8651: Turn to entry 152.
EH 53 R 9542: Turn to entry 74.

112 That path won't take you anywhere good! Lose a life, and find your way back to entry 51.

113 That rope will not take you down to where the bomb is. Lose a life, and climb back up to entry 90.

You worked out the correct combination and opened the briefcase. Inside it you find the name of a famous monument—the next one that Agent 9 intends to destroy. It's been written in a letter substitution code.

HDVWHU LVODQG PRDL VWDWXHV

Which of these monuments is Agent 9's next target?

If your answer is a famous bridge in San Francisco, turn to entry 42.

If your answer is a wobbly tower in Pisa, turn to entry 133.

If your answer is the longest wall in the world, turn to entry 66.

If your answer is the statues on a Pacific island, turn to entry 203.

115 That is not Rochelle Blake. Lose a life, and head back to entry 54.

116 That's not what the coded message said. Lose a life, and decrypt your way back to entry 190.

117

You descend in the elevator and enter the lobby, then the war room. There are four doors, one leading to the living quarters, with access to the rest of the lair. The other three lead to rooms where you will either be imprisoned or interrogated. Unfortunately, the map doesn't make clear which door leads where.

Each door is marked with a snowflake symbol. One of these matches the torn snowflake on your map of Greenland. That's the door you must take. Can you work out which one it is?

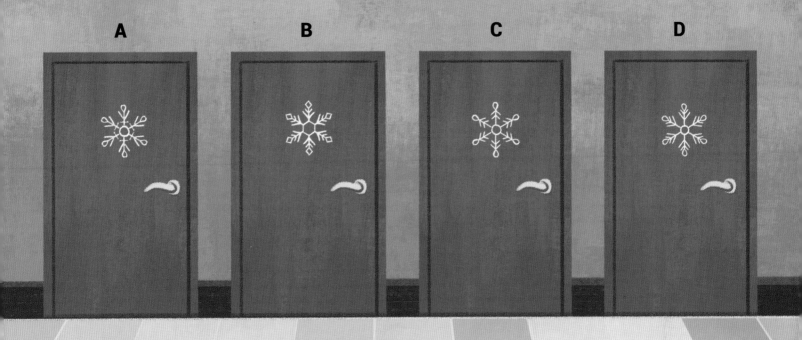

If you think it's A, turn to entry 153.
If you think it's B, turn to entry 81.
If you think it's C, turn to entry 104.
If you think it's D, turn to entry 68.

118
That is not the correct phone number. Lose a life, and dial back to entry 100.

119
That is not Agent 9's next target. Lose a life, and head back to entry 32.

You reach Machu Picchu with just minutes to spare. You find the bomb in the Temple of the Three Windows, and now you must deactivate it by solving the numerical puzzle on the bomb.

$9 \times 40 \div 4 + 56 - 9 =$

What's the answer?
If you think it's 148, turn to entry 83.
If you think it's 137, turn to entry 131.
If you think it's 129, turn to entry 12.
If you think it's 151, turn to entry 156.

121 Air Guanaco is not the quickest flight to Peru. Lose a life, and soar back to entry 148.

122 That combination will not result in the right answer. Lose a life, and recalculate your way back to entry 75.

123 Your calculations are wrong! Lose a life, have another think, and go back to entry 72.

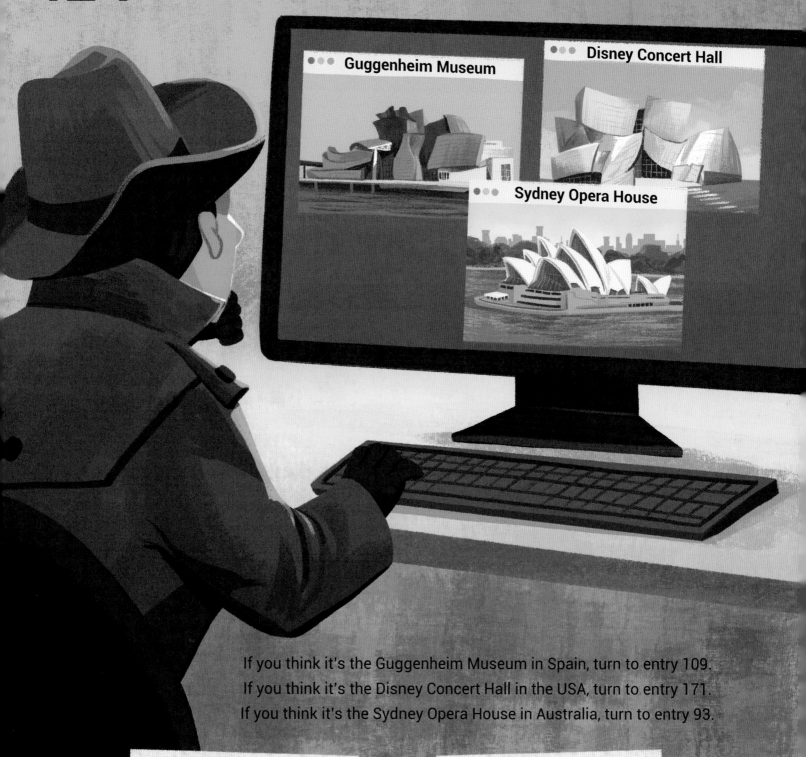

124

The picture is of a very famous building. Could this be Agent 9's next target? You consult E.A.G.L.E.'s database. What is this building, and where in the world is it?

Guggenheim Museum

Disney Concert Hall

Sydney Opera House

If you think it's the Guggenheim Museum in Spain, turn to entry 109.

If you think it's the Disney Concert Hall in the USA, turn to entry 171.

If you think it's the Sydney Opera House in Australia, turn to entry 93.

125 You won't get to the overhead compartment in time. Lose a life, and jump back down to entry 169.

126 That message is not correctly coded. Manuel will smell a fish! Lose a life, and go back to entry 79.

127

You have worked out where Agent 9 is sitting. Now Ridley Crow disguises himself as a train steward to see if he can damage Agent 9's phone, to stop him from setting off the bomb by remote control. You hack into the train's CCTV to see how Ridley is getting on, but it's been badly corrupted by Agent 9's scrambler, and there are just six film stills left. Can you put them in the right order?

Which order is correct?

4, 5, 6, 1, 2, 3: turn to entry 91.

3, 5, 1, 4, 6, 2: turn to entry 162.

6, 1, 5, 4, 3, 2: turn to entry 108.

2, 4, 6, 5, 1, 3: turn to entry 47.

128
The driver is not Freddy Ravelo. Lose a life, and reverse back to entry 86.

129
That flight is not the quickest. Lose a life, and jet back to entry 93.

130
That is not an anagram of Astra Celeste. Lose a life, and unscramble your way back to entry 18.

131

You've succeeded in deactivating the bomb. But there may still be others. Agent 9 has raced back to his top secret lair—an abandoned military base buried deep under the Greenland ice. This is where he controls his deadly satellite laser gun.

Ridley Crow gives you a map, showing you where it is. Solve the riddle to work out the coordinates of Agent 9's lair.

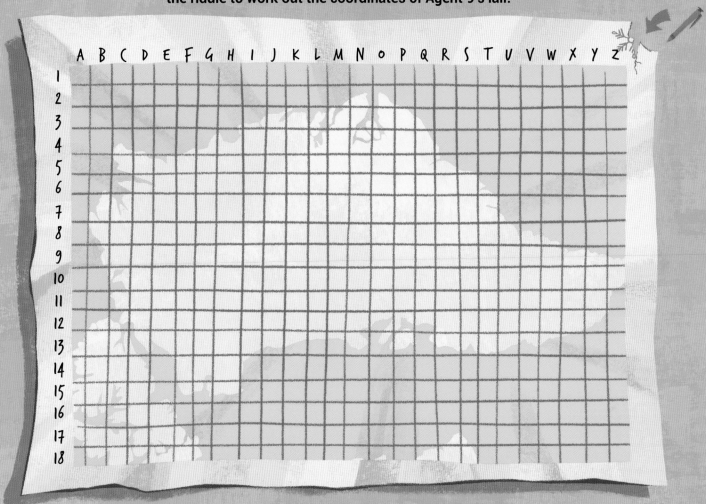

Clues:

The letter is in RASCAL and SCOUNDREL but not in WASTREL.

The number is in 7-10-4-8-13-6 and in 6-8-4-13-7-10 but not in 13-4-6-10-2-7.

If you think the coordinates are C8, turn to entry 54.

If you think the coordinates are R10, turn to entry 188.

If you think the coordinates are L4, turn to entry 22.

If you think the coordinates are H12, turn to entry 49.

132
That fuse does not lead to the dynamite. Lose a life, and detonate yourself back to entry 177.

133
You're leaning the wrong way with that one! Lose a life, and go back to entry 114.

134

You and Astra Celeste find your way to the Control Room. You overpower Agent 9 and tie him up, but he laughs: "The clock is ticking down before the laser activates the next bomb. You haven't got time to deactivate it."

Astra tells you that the deactivation code is the year Agent 9 turned 21. Luckily, she knows a few details about his family history: Agent 9 was born four years after his brother. His brother is ten years older than his sister. His sister turned 12 in 2010.

ENTER CODE

☐ ☐ ☐ ☐

So what is the code?

A 2011: turn to entry 101.

B 2012: turn to entry 26.

C 2013: turn to entry 193.

D 2014: turn to entry 139.

135 Those are not the coordinates of the bomb's location. Lose a life, and dash back to entry 58.

136 The book you're looking for is not on that shelf. Lose a life, and turn back to entry 155.

137 That combination will not open the briefcase. Lose a life, and go back to entry 61.

138

You successfully disguise yourself as Rochelle Blake and sneak past the guards. You are now outside the entrance of Agent 9's lair. You ditch the disguise and examine the code panel. Ridley Crow told you the code word to gain entry is AGENT. In what order should you press the buttons?

1	B	R	E	C	U
2	A	S	M	I	D
3	Q	L	Z	K	T
4	Y	G	P	V	O
5	J	W	X	N	H

If you think the code is 1-3-5-2-4, turn to entry 145.

If you think the code is 2-4-1-5-3, turn to entry 117.

If you think the code is 4-5-2-3-1, turn to entry 88.

139 That is not the right answer. Lose a life, work on that sum again, and return to entry 134.

140 Sorry, but you got that one wrong. Lose a life, and return to entry 107.

141

You have successfully deduced the bomb deactivation code. You have only 40 minutes left before it's due to go off. To save time, you rent a helicopter and fly there, but there are several possible places to land. Agent 9 is trying to confuse you with holograms! Which of these buildings is the real Taj Mahal?

A

B

C

If you think it's A, turn to entry 191.

If you think it's B, turn to entry 166.

If you think it's C, turn to entry 24.

142 That is not Manuel Malado you see through the window. Lose a life, and edge your way back to entry 82.

143 That is not the next shape in the pattern sequence. Lose a life, and puzzle your way back to entry 64.

144

Phew! You managed to deactivate the bomb and save the moai of Easter Island. However, when you return to New York City, you hear that Agent 9 has picked a new target to attack.

You receive a communiqué from E.A.G.L.E. command. You are to meet with another agent. He walks his dog through Central Park every day at 5 o'clock.
Can you identify him from the following encoded description?

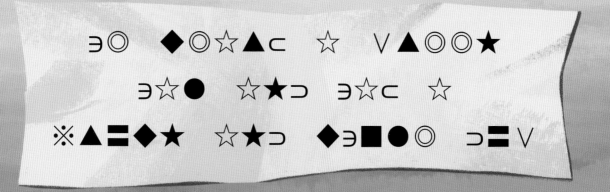

If you think it's A, turn to entry 21.

If you think it's B, turn to entry 105.

If you think it's C, turn to entry 89.

145 That code combination will not get you into Agent 9's lair. Lose a life, and go back to entry 138.

146 The bus is not the quickest way of getting to the Opera House. Lose a life, and ride back to entry 40.

147 That route is not the quickest. Lose a life, and talk your way back to entry 68.

148 You are correct. Agent 9's next bomb attack will be on the famous Inca citadel of Machu Picchu in Peru. You check flights from Cairo to the Peruvian city of Puno. The trip will take 25 hours, not including stops. The quickest flight will get you there by 5.15 pm the next day. Can you work out which one it is?

DEPARTURES

Airline	Depart	Stop 1: Paris	Stop 2: Lima
Llama Airways	2.30 pm	1 hour	75 minutes
Camel Airlines	3 pm	45 minutes	30 minutes
Alpaca Air	2 pm	90 minutes	1 hour
Air Guanaco	2.45 pm	75 minutes	45 minutes

If you think it's Llama Airways, turn to entry 176.
If you think it's Camel Airlines, turn to entry 86.
If you think it's Alpaca Air, turn to entry 20.
If you think it's Air Guanaco, turn to entry 121.

149 That monument is not the Arc de Triomphe. Lose a life, and go back to entry 21.

150 That is not the boat's name. Lose a life, and sail back to entry 203.

151 That fuse does not lead to the bomb. Lose a life, and blast your way back to entry 177.

152

You manage to figure out the registration number, and with the help of the police, you track down the car in a parking lot in the city of Agra, where the Taj Mahal is located.

The car is abandoned, but you find a fingerprint on the steering wheel.
You check it against the E.A.G.L.E. database. Who does it belong to?

Name: Agent 9
Eyes: Blue
Height: 170 cm

Name: Ridley Crow
Eyes: Brown
Height: 185 cm

Name: Astra Celeste
Eyes: Brown
Height: 165 cm

If you think the fingerprint belongs to Agent 9, turn to entry 196.

If you think the fingerprint belongs to Ridley Crow, turn to entry 7.

If you think the fingerprint belongs to Astra Celeste, turn to entry 62.

153 That is not the correct snowflake design. Lose a life, and shiver your way back to entry 117.

154 Stonehenge is not the right monument! Lose a life, and decode your way back to entry 187.

You make it through the labyrinth. A set of stairs takes you into a library. Ridley says he remembers Agent 9 telling him he's hidden a vital secret in a book with a five-word title containing the following letters: A, W, T, V, Y. Is it on shelf A, B, C, or D?

If you think the book is on Shelf A, turn to entry 136.

If you think the book is on Shelf B, turn to entry 2.

If you think the book is on Shelf C, turn to entry 179.

If you think the book is on Shelf D, turn to entry 44.

156 That number will not deactivate the bomb. Lose a life, and detonate yourself back to entry 120.

157 That is not the odd tile. You'll need to keep looking. Lose a life, and head back to entry 163.

158 That is the wrong answer. Lose a life, and head back across the lake to entry 25.

You correctly identify the location of the bomb. Now you have to get there. Also in the envelope are two sets of train and bus tickets to Machu Picchu, and a note in symbol code.

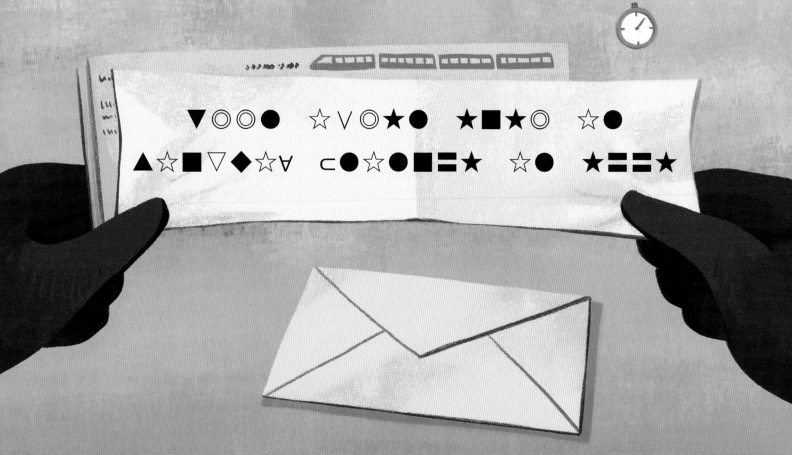

What do you think it says?

Catch Madison Blair and let Agent Nine know. Turn to entry 201.

Take train to Machu Picchu and await further orders. Turn to entry 194.

Meet Agent Nine at Railway Station at noon. Turn to entry 79.

160 That is not the name of the boat. Lose a life, and set sail back to entry 203.

161 That was not the woman you saw. Lose a life, and go back to entry 173.

162 That is not the correct order of the film stills. Lose a life, and reshuffle your way back to entry 127.

163

You correctly identify the CCTV image that shows Agent 9. You track his movements after he leaves the parking lot via CCTV, and you discover that he lives in a nearby house, under the name Oberon Fitzpatrick. You pay him a visit. A butler shows you into a large room. Suddenly, you fall through a trapdoor into a basement.

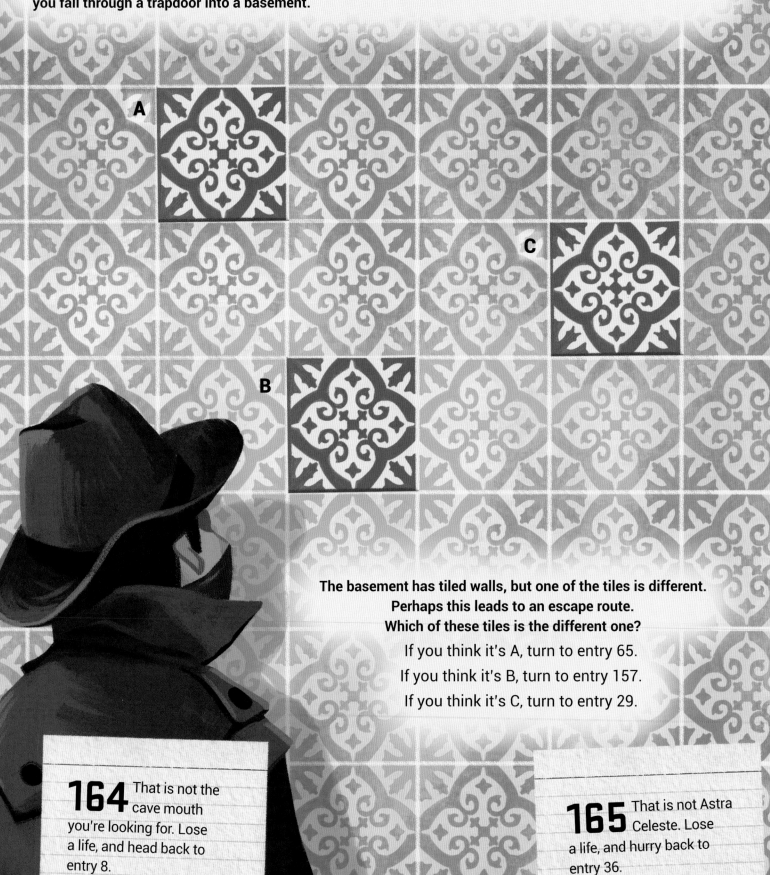

The basement has tiled walls, but one of the tiles is different.
Perhaps this leads to an escape route.
Which of these tiles is the different one?

If you think it's A, turn to entry 65.

If you think it's B, turn to entry 157.

If you think it's C, turn to entry 29.

164 That is not the cave mouth you're looking for. Lose a life, and head back to entry 8.

165 That is not Astra Celeste. Lose a life, and hurry back to entry 36.

You've found the right building. After landing the helicopter in the grounds, you run inside the mausoleum. You have just three minutes left to find the bomb and deactivate it.

In the library book was a photo that gave you a clue as to the bomb's location—a close-up picture of where Agent 9 has hidden the bomb. Can you match the close-up picture to the part of the room where the bomb is?

If you think it's A, turn to entry 92.

If you think it's B, turn to entry 202.

If you think it's C, turn to entry 177.

167 That combination will not get you to the required answer. Dust off that calculator, lose a life, and head back to entry 75.

168 Those numbers will not open your handcuffs. Lose a life, and recalculate your way back to entry 183.

169

You are right: it's Ridley Crow. You bang on the window and he helps you in. Agent 9 is about to enter the carriage in search of you. You have four possible hiding places. Which can you get to the fastest, if you run at 5 paces a second?

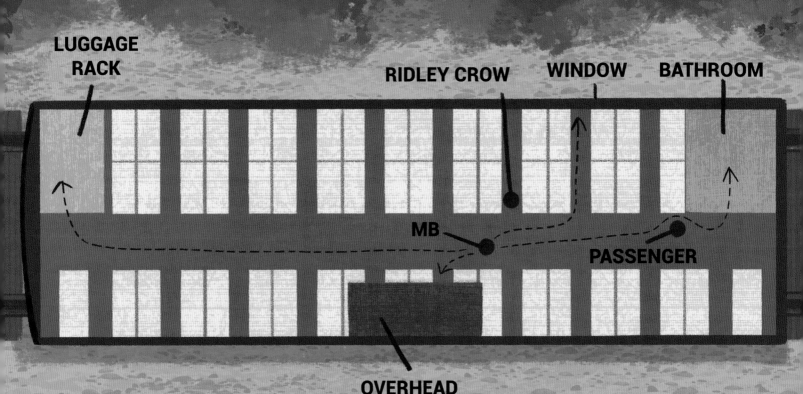

LUGGAGE RACK

RIDLEY CROW **WINDOW** **BATHROOM**

MB

PASSENGER

OVERHEAD COMPARTMENT GAP

Bathroom 30 paces away, but someone's blocking the aisle, costing you 4 extra seconds: turn to entry 184.

Climb back out the window 12 seconds: turn to entry 52.

Luggage rack 45 paces away: turn to entry 11.

Gap in overhead compartment 25 paces away, plus 6 seconds to get up there: turn to entry 125.

170 That is not where Agent 9 is sitting. Lose a life, and make your way back to entry 97.

171 That building is not on Agent 9's hitlist. Lose a life, and return to entry 124.

172 Those are not the coordinates of the bomb's location. Lose a life, and hurry back to entry 58.

173

You get to Joe Brown Café at 11 am. It's full of people. You look around in search of the woman you saw by the opera house. She has changed her outfit but you recognize her shoes. Which of these people is it?

If your answer is A, turn to entry 107.
If your answer is B, turn to entry 161.
If your answer is C, turn to entry 84.

174 That is not the quickest route to Machu Picchu. Lose a life, and whirl back to entry 47.

175 Sorry, but that's the wrong answer. Lose a life, and go back to entry 107.

176 Llama Airways is not the quickest flight to Peru. Lose a life, and fly back to entry 148.

177

Congratulations! You found the earthquake bomb and used the code to deactivate it, but then you see Agent 9. "You may have defused my earthquake bomb," he crows, "but can you save yourself from old-fashioned dynamite?" There are three fuses, all burning. Which one leads to the dynamite?

A
B
C
D

If you think it's A, turn to entry 151.

If you think it's B, turn to entry 187.

If you think it's C, turn to entry 14.

If you think it's D, turn to entry 132.

178
That is not the correct phone number. Lose a life, and call back to entry 100.

179
The book you're searching for is not on that shelf. Lose a life, and turn the page back to entry 155.

180

You manage to unscramble Astra's name and you call her on her burner phone. She says she has information and will meet you at Cairo Airport. You are met by three women claiming to be Astra. Two must be enemy agents in disguise!

Thinking fast, you remember something you observed when you met Astra in the café.

You ask them, "How do you take your coffee?"

"Milk and one sugar," replies the one on the left.

"Black, no sugar," replies the one in the middle.

"Milk and no sugar," replies the one on the right.

Which one is Astra?

If you think it's A, turn to entry 186.

If you think it's B, turn to entry 5.

If you think it's C, turn to entry 71.

181
That is not what the agent is wearing. Lose a life, and decode your way back to entry 190.

182
That is not the correct monument. Lose a life, and go back to entry 21.

183

You work out that the man who has captured you is Manuel Malado. As he drives away, you study your handcuffs. They have a four-digit combination lock. You try to remember the number on the lock when he opened them to put on your wrists.

You remember the following:

- There was no 7, 4, 1, or 9.
- The numbers went even, odd, even, odd.
- The first number was one higher than the second and a lower number than the third.
- No numbers were repeated.

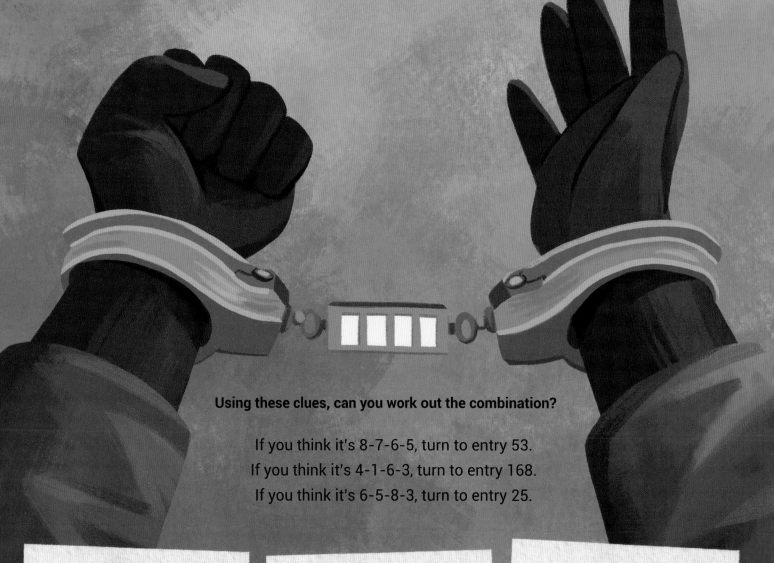

Using these clues, can you work out the combination?

If you think it's 8-7-6-5, turn to entry 53.
If you think it's 4-1-6-3, turn to entry 168.
If you think it's 6-5-8-3, turn to entry 25.

184 The bathroom is not a good choice. Agent 9 will see you before you get there. Lose a life, and return to entry 169.

185 No, that's not the right building. Lose a life, and go back to entry 1.

186 That is not Astra Celeste, so please do not say "hello" to her! Lose a life, and head back to entry 180.

187

Well done! You've managed to defuse the dynamite. But Agent 9 is nowhere to be seen. Outside the Taj Mahal you spot a note he dropped that he must have been planning to pass on to his assistant. It includes the name of his next target. Can you crack the symbol code to work out what it is?

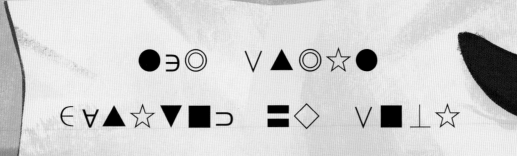

Crack the code and decide which of these famous monuments the note refers to:

If you think it is a vibrant cathedral in Moscow, Russia, turn to entry 46.

If you think it is a prehistoric group of standing stones in Wiltshire, UK, turn to entry 154.

If you think it is an ancient temple on the Acropolis, Greece, turn to entry 69.

If you think it is an ancient, triangular structure in Egypt, turn to entry 18.

188 Those are the wrong coordinates. Lose a life, and navigate your way back to entry 131.

189 That is not the symbol on the broken tile. Lose a life, and go back to entry 29.

190

You reach the Great Pyramid by the quickest route, and are relieved to see it's still standing! You look at the message Astra gave you. She said it would help you identify the T.H.O.R.N. agent placing the bomb. Some of it is in a code that substitutes letters for numbers. Can you decode it?

The agent is in a 7-18-5-5-14 or 2-12-21-5 hat, 15-18-1-14-7-5 shorts, a 23-8-9-20-5 or 25-5-12-12-15-23 top, and has a 3-1-13-5-18-1.

Which answer is correct? The T.H.O.R.N. agent is in a ...

- straw or panama hat, long shorts, a green or purple top, and has a beard. Turn to entry 181.
- cowboy or sailor hat, flowery shorts, a red or green top, and has a briefcase. Turn to entry 4.
- green or blue hat, orange shorts, a white or yellow top, and has a camera. Turn to entry 15.
- fedora or derby hat, dark shorts, a stained or ripped top, and has a gun. Turn to entry 116.

191 That is not the Taj Mahal. Lose a life, and fly back to entry 141.

192 That airline won't get you there the quickest. Lose a life, and fly back to entry 93.

193

Congratulations! You have deactivated the laser weapon, and have foiled Agent 9's evil plans to destroy the world's most-famous monuments!

You call in the police, and Agent 9 and his accomplices are arrested and taken away. Thanks to your efforts, the Easter Island moai, the Taj Mahal, the Great Pyramid of Giza, and Machu Picchu are all still standing.

194 You may need to work on your code-busting skills! Lose a life, and return to entry 159.

195 The agent is not in that square. Lose a life, and shoot back to entry 15.

196 You have identified the fingerprint as belonging to Agent 9. That means your enemy is in this city, and he captured Ridley Crow. You check the CCTV footage from the parking lot. Aware that he could be in disguise, you carefully study the posture, height, and body shape of three possible suspects. Which one of these people could be Agent 9?

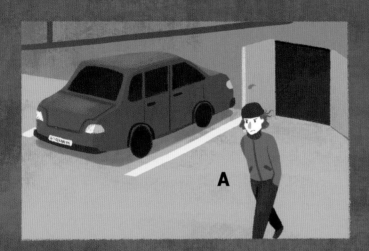

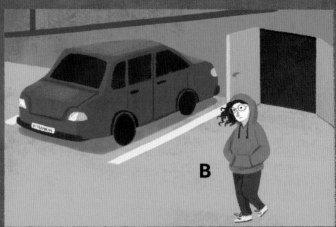

If you think it's A, turn to entry 163.
If you think it's B, turn to entry 59.
If you think it's C, turn to entry 43.

197 That is not Agent 9's next target. Lose a life, and make your way back to entry 32.

198 That is not the car's registration number. Lose a life, and motor your way back to entry 111.

199

You correctly calculate that Manuel will catch up with you in 15 minutes, so you make landfall after 12 minutes and head back into town.

The envelope you stole contains part of a map of Machu Picchu with a cross on it. This has to be where the bomb has been placed. Can you find this area on the main map?

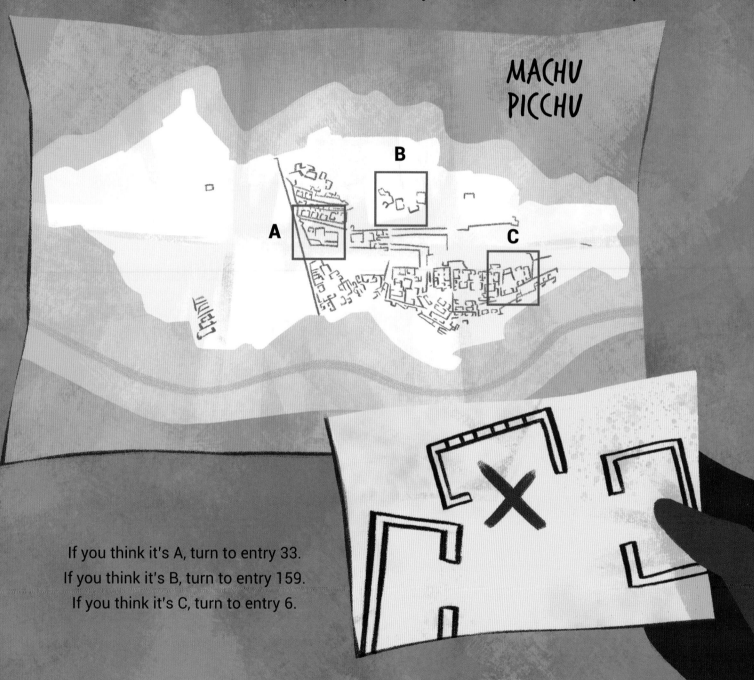

MACHU PICCHU

B

A

C

If you think it's A, turn to entry 33.

If you think it's B, turn to entry 159.

If you think it's C, turn to entry 6.

200 That is not the correct bomb deactivation code. Lose a life, and blast your way back to entry 44.

201 That is not what the message says. Lose a life, and decode your way back to entry 159.

202 That is not where the bomb is hidden. Lose a life, and go back to entry 166.

203 You correctly worked out that Agent 9's next target is the famous moai statues of Easter Island in the Pacific Ocean. You immediately fly there in search of the bomb. There are only 24 hours to go before it is detonated.

At the island's main town of Hanga Roa, you question people at the docks. A fisherman says a man with long red hair borrowed one of the boats recently, but he can't remember the boat's name. Work out the name from this clue: He tells you he thinks the name has a "K" and an "N" but no "E."

KALENGA

TARAKAI

TONGARIKI

RARAKU

204 That is not the correct missing piece of the photograph. Lose a life, and shoot back to entry 11.

If your answer is Kalenga, turn to entry 150.
If your answer is Tarakai, turn to entry 45.
If your answer is Tongariki, turn to entry 8.
If your answer is Raraku, turn to entry 160.

205 You've ended up in the wrong café. Lose a life, have a milkshake, and return to entry 103.

206 That is not the next shape in the pattern sequence. Lose a life, and think your way back to entry 64.